First World War
and Army of Occupation
War Diary
France, Belgium and Germany

GUARDS DIVISION
1 Guards Brigade
Headquarters
1 June 1917 - 30 June 1917

WO95/1213/9

The Naval & Military Press Ltd
www.nmarchive.com
Published in association with The National Archives

Published by

The Naval & Military Press Ltd

Unit 10 Ridgewood Industrial Park,
Uckfield, East Sussex,
TN22 5QE England
Tel: +44 (0) 1825 749494

www.naval-military-press.com

www.nmarchive.com

This diary has been reprinted in facsimile from the original. Any imperfections are inevitably reproduced and the quality may fall short of modern type and cartographic standards.

© **Crown Copyright**
Images reproduced by permission of The National Archives, London, England, 2015.

Contents

Document type	Place/Title	Date From	Date To
Heading	WO95/1213 June 1917.		
War Diary	Renescure	01/06/1917	10/06/1917
War Diary	Renescure	07/06/1917	16/06/1917
War Diary	Renescure To Winnizeele	16/06/1917	16/06/1917
War Diary	Winnizeele To Proven Area	17/06/1917	19/06/1917
War Diary	F.15.c Central Sheet 27.	20/06/1917	24/06/1917
War Diary	F.15.c. Central To A.4.d.9.2 (Sheet 28)	25/06/1917	27/06/1917
War Diary	A.4.d.9.2	28/06/1917	28/06/1917
War Diary	A.4.d.9.2 to Elverdimghe Chateau	29/06/1917	30/06/1917
Miscellaneous	1st Guards Brigade Conference-June 2nd, 1917.	02/06/1917	02/06/1917
Miscellaneous	Officers And Other Ranks To Be Left Behind In An Attack.		
Miscellaneous	2nd. Battalion Grenadier Guards. Shooting Averages.	15/06/1917	15/06/1917
Heading	Bde HQ		
Miscellaneous	2nd Battalion Coldstream Guards. Best Shooting Company Competition 11-12th June 1917.	11/06/1917	11/06/1917
Miscellaneous			
Miscellaneous	1st Guards Bde.	13/06/1917	13/06/1917
Miscellaneous	3rd Battalion Coldstream Guards	11/06/1917	11/06/1917
Miscellaneous	3rd Battalion Coldstream Guards.	12/06/1917	12/06/1917
Miscellaneous	1st Battn. Irish Guards.	14/06/1917	14/06/1917
Operation(al) Order(s)	1st Guards Brigade Order No. 125.	07/06/1917	07/06/1917
Miscellaneous	March Table.		
Operation(al) Order(s)	Supplement to 1st Guards Brigade Order No. 125.	09/06/1917	09/06/1917
Operation(al) Order(s)	1st Guards Brigade Order No. 126.	15/06/1917	15/06/1917
Miscellaneous	March Table.		
Operation(al) Order(s)	1st Guards Brigade Order No. 127.	16/06/1917	16/06/1917
Miscellaneous	March Table.		
Miscellaneous	1st G.B. No. 1239.	20/06/1917	20/06/1917
Operation(al) Order(s)	1st Guards Brigade Order No. 128.	20/06/1917	20/06/1917
Operation(al) Order(s)	1st Guards Brigade Order No. 129.	24/06/1917	24/06/1917
Operation(al) Order(s)	March Table To 1st Guards Brigade Order No. 129.		
Miscellaneous	2nd Bn. Grenadier Guards. 2nd Bn. Coldstream Guards.	26/06/1917	26/06/1917
Miscellaneous	1st Guards Bde Defence Scheme Provisional.		
Miscellaneous	Appendix "A". Principles Of Defence.		
Miscellaneous	Appendix "B". Dispositions Of Machine Guns.		
Miscellaneous	Appendix "D" Gas Attack And "Wind Dangerous" Period.		
Operation(al) Order(s)	1st Guards Brigade Order No. 130.	27/06/1917	27/06/1917
Miscellaneous			
Miscellaneous	Intelligence Report-1st Guards Brigade. 11 a.m. June 29th to 11 a.m. June 30th.	29/06/1917	29/06/1917

WO 95
12-13
June 1917

WAR DIARY or **INTELLIGENCE SUMMARY**   Army Form C. 2118

Headquarters 1st Guards Brigade   June 1917

Vol 23

Place	Date	Hour	Summary of Events and Information	Remarks and references to Appendices
RENESCURE.	June 1st	2 pm	Arrival of the Bde Group in RENESCURE area completed.	
	June 2nd	12 noon	Brigadier held a conference of commanding officers to points discussed at Div H.Q.	Appx 363
		11 am	Conference held at Div H.Q. chiefly with a view to arranging details of Div Concentration.	
ditto	June 3rd to June 10th		The ground available for training was limited to a field for each Bn. & the Bn. & Coy & CLAIRMARAIS wood for all units. The result was that training was confined to drill — musketry — specialist training & drill — objects being marked out with tape. The object of their attacks was to train trenches to trench attacks in a field — objects being marked out with tape. The object of their attacks was to train subordinate commanders to think & out their dispositions & formations for the attack & to accustom all ranks to know exactly where he had to go & when & how — & what to do when he got there. The following officers of the Bde Staff were mentioned in the Birthday Honors Gaz Brig Gen. E.D. JEFFREYS. C.M.G. (appointed Brevet Colonel) Capt. Bn. R. BECKWITH-SMITH D.S.O. received Military Cross J.B.C. & A. A.D.S.S/Forms/C.2118. Capt. G.G. EVANS M.C. (Staff Capt) mentioned in despatches	

Army Form C. 2118

WAR DIARY
or
INTELLIGENCE SUMMARY
(Erase heading not required.)

Instructions regarding War Diaries and Intelligence Summaries are contained in F.S. Regs., Part II. and the Staff Manual respectively. Title Pages will be prepared in manuscript.

Place	Date	Hour	Summary of Events and Information	Remarks and references to Appendices
RENESCURE	June 7th	8/am	1st Bn Batt Order No 125 - issued all ranks confined to Div area -	Appx 364.
	June 10th	6/am	Conference at Div H.Q. on training future. On this date 2nd and 3rd Coldstream Gds moved as per appx 354 to practise musketry.	
	June 13th		2nd Bn Gren Gds & 1st Bn Irish Gds moved as per appx 354 to relieve 2nd & 3rd Bns Coldstream Gds on practise musketry, 2nd & 3rd Bns Coldstream Gds returning to RENESCURE area. The musketry practise obtained was necessary to keep up - the weather was fine & Bns shot well considering the rust away from practise, they had had cleaning the back bone. The chief fault which in the rapid & magazine was that men fired to the the first pull off - Instructors watched the target instead of the men.	

WAR DIARY or INTELLIGENCE SUMMARY

Army Form C. 2118

Place	Date	Hour	Summary of Events and Information	Remarks and references to Appendices
RENESCURE	June 14th		2nd Bn. Gren Gds. to 1st Bn. Irish Gds. returned to RENESCURE area.	
"	June 15th	2 pm	Orders received that Bde would move following day to WINNIZEELE area.	Appx 385.
"		5 pm	1st Gds. Bde. Order 126 issued.	
" to WINNIZEELE	June 16th	8 am	Head of column passed S.P. The day turned out to be an extremely hot one — units of the 1st Gds Bde front all marched well with the exception of 2nd Coldstream of whom a large number fell out. 2nd Bn. Gren Gds. to 50th Field Coy having an extra long march halted for several hours till cool of evening.	Appx 386
		4 pm	1st Gds Bde Order No 127 issued. Bde H.Q. 2nd Bn. Gren Gds. 2nd Bn. Coldm. Gds. 3rd Bn. Coldm. Gds. Bde in billets as follows: WINNIZEELE area. 1st Bn. Irish Gds. OUDEZEELE area. 2nd F A	

WAR DIARY or INTELLIGENCE SUMMARY

Army Form C. 2118.

Place	Date	Hour	Summary of Events and Information	Remarks and references to Appendices
WINNIZEELE to PROVEN area	June 17th	8am	Head of column passed S.P. in accordance with app 366. The day was again an extremely hot one but the march was a comparatively short one - only about 3 men in the Bde fell out. The area into which the Bde marched was already full of troops & the Bde was accommodated in tents & bivouacs. Bde H.Q. had one room in a farm house at F.15.c. central for a Bde office. Remainder of Bde was in area F.9. F.14. F.15. (Sheet 27) (Sheet 28)	
	June 18th		3rd Coldstream Bn moved to A.10.c. bivouacs to work under O.C. Gds Sigs on buried cable. 2nd Bn Gren Gds having received an extra day in WINNIZEELE area moved up & occupied the camp vacated by 3rd Coldstream Bn.	
		6pm	Conference at Div H.Q. on future operations. 2.5.O.R.R from Bde attached to 75th Field Coy until further orders.	
	June 19th		Various fatigues had to be found daily from the state amounting to about 3 companies - & no that training progress - being all cultivated ground - no that training was confined to drill - musketry - route marching.	

Place	Date	Hour	Summary of Events and Information	Remarks and references to Appendices
F.15.c (also sheet 2)	June 20.		2nd Bn. Grenadier Gds & 2nd Bn. Coldstream Gds attended a ceremonial parade at HERZEELE when General ANTOINE commanding 1st French Army presented the Legion of Honour to about 45 British Officers. Two French Bns also attended the parade. Bns were drawn up in three sides of a square in mass (two Bns in the centre face of the square) French Bns on the right - British Bns on the left Battalions were inspected by Gen Gough (comm. 5th English Army) - after the presentation of Decorations Bns marched past in columns of platoons. Defence Scheme for Role in Div reserve issued. 1st Gds Role Order No.127 issued. Casualties 3rd Bn. Coldstream Gds. O.R. wounded 9. with night working party near ELVERDINGHE	App 367 App 368
	June 21st A.B"		Orders received for Role to move further forward on June 23rd	

WAR DIARY or INTELLIGENCE SUMMARY

Army Form C. 2118.

Place	Date	Hour	Summary of Events and Information	Remarks and references to Appendices
F.15.c central (Sheet 2)	June 24th		2nd Bn. Grenadier Gds. moved to DE WIPPE CABARET cross roads & took over cable burying fatigue being done by 3rd Coldstream. 3rd Coldstream did not move as previously ordered in rifle Bde Order No 110. The St. Anne Commander visited Bde H.Q. 1st Bde Order No 129 issued.	App 369
F.15.c central to A.4.d.9.2 (Sheet 28)	June 25th		The Bde less 2nd Bn. Gren. Gds. moved in accordance with Order 129.	
	June 26th		Various fatigues were found by the Bde. 1st Bde Provisional defence scheme issued for study by units before going into the line. Casualties. 2nd Gren Gds 1 O.R. wounded at duty.	App 370
	June 27th		1st Rifle Bde Order No 130 issued. From June 17th up to this date 2000 men had to be found. This figure amounting to very nearly 2000 men per day. In this A.G.O area the nature of the country prevented any extensive training being carried out. The enemy had taken to doing a certain amount of shelling with long range guns of this shelling was done at night & for the most part directed at rest of this road & railways	App 371

WAR DIARY or INTELLIGENCE SUMMARY

Army Form C. 2118.

Place	Date	Hour	Summary of Events and Information	Remarks and references to Appendices
A.4.d.9.2.	June 28th		1st Irish Gds moved to ROUSSEL Farm. 3rd Coldstream relieved 3rd Bde T.M.By Green Gds in front line of BOESINGHE sector. 1st Gds Bde T.M. By. relieved 2nd Gds Bde T.M. By. 3 days relief passed off fairly quietly & without casualties.	
A.4.d.9.2 to ELVERDINGHE CHATEAU	June 29th		2nd Coldstream relieved 2nd Irish Gds in support. 2nd Bde Green Gds moved to CARDOEN Farm. Bde H.Q. moved to ELVERDINGHE Chateau – G.O.C. 1st Gds Bde taking over command owing to shelling of Batteries by 5.9 Hoo + H.V. guns at the night time a very noisy one in vicinity of Bde H.Q. but fairly quiet in the line.	Intelligence App. 372
	June 30th		A quiet day – probably owing to heavy rain. Casualties 10 to 12 noon. 2nd Colds Gds O.R. killed 1 " " wounded 5 3rd Colds Gds O.R. " 1 1st Irish Gds " " 1 1st Gds Bde T.M. By – " wounded 4 Batteries in vicinity of Bde H.Q. shelled during evening + night.	

J.S. Jefferys
Commdg 1st Gds Bde
1.7.17.

1st G.B. No.955.

1st Guards Brigade Conference - June 2nd, 1917.

1. The Brigadier emphasised that owing to the limited ground for training, attention must be paid to -

   (a) Drill, especially arm drill by numbers.

   (b) Route marching. Short marches to be done (men carrying packs) to some place where drill, musketry, or some other form of training, can be done.

   (c) Elementary musketry.

   (d) Bombing and Rifle Grenade work. Instruction should always be carried out with some definite aiming point. Bombers should receive special training in throwing. Attention was drawn to Brigade Order No.329 of May 28th, 1917, 're' Selection of men for Brigade Bombing Courses.

   (e) Lewis Gun instruction.

   (f) CLAIRMARAIS Wood is the only ground of any extent available for training.

   The N.E. quarter is allotted to 3/C.G.)
   " N.W.   "   "   "   "   1/I.G.)
   " S.W.   "   "   "   "   2/G.G.) daily.
   " S.E.   "   "   "   "   2/C.G.)

   Wood-fighting should be practised in accordance with Infantry Training, Section 154.

2. The Brigadier directed that Battalion Courses for the training of instructors in musketry, bayonet fighting, and bombing and rifle grenades, be continued. In the musketry courses instruction must be given on the Hythe Lines and instructors must be taught to correct mistakes.

3. Brigade Bayonet Fighting (for advanced training of instructors) and Bombing Courses will be started as soon as possible.

   Lieut., C.J. HAMBRO will replace Lieut. R.V.J. CARINGTON as Brigade Bombing Officer while the latter is on leave. Lieut. HAMBRO is required to report at Brigade H.Q., on June 4th.

4. It is possible that Battalions may be sent to near TATINGHEM to do two days shooting on the range.

   If leave can be obtained, a short range for each Battn., will be dug in CLAIRMARAIS Wood.

P.T.O.

(2)

5. The Brigadier drew attention to S.S.180 - "Experiences of a Division in Recent Fighting", and asked C.O's to draw the attention of all Subordinates to this pamphlet.

6. Battalions were asked to send in a return of Signallers now present with Battalions.

The Brigadier directed that if Battalions have a good Signalling Officer he is to be appointed Battalion Signalling Officer.

7. The actual Officers and numbers of Other Ranks to be left behind in the event of the Division taking part in an attack was discussed. A separate list is attached.
Units were asked to send in the names of Officers whom it is intended to leave out and the approximate number of Other Ranks.

8. O.C's were asked to see that their Units were in possession of all necessary equipment such as Rifle Grenade Haversacks, wire cutters, very pistols, etc.,

9. The Brigadier directed that the Rev: C. LYTTELTON should be attached to 2nd Bn. Grenadier Guards from today, and that the Rev: H. HUBBARD to the 2nd or 3rd Bn. Coldstream Guards from the 4th inst., O.C., 2nd and 3rd Coldstream Guards to decide between them which and inform this Office by tomorrow night.

10. The Brigadier drew attention to the Divnl. Competition and asked Units to paint their vehicles and polish up their harness.

11. The Brigadier explained the working of the Officers Leave Roster.

12. Units were asked to send in Training Programmes by 8 p.m. daily. This may be done by wire.

Captain,

2nd June 1917. Brigade Major, 1st Guards Brigade.

Officers and Other Ranks to be left behind in an Attack.

BATTALIONS.

Officers.
2nd in Command.
Adjutant or Adjutants understudy.
----
2 Company Commanders (one of which will *go in with* Bn. H.Q.,)
2 Officers next for Command of Companies.
Such other Officers as are required to bring the number taken into action down to 75% of the total number in the Battalion and below 20 in all: very young Regular Officers to be preferably left.

Other Ranks.
Regtl. Sergt. Major and 1 Drill Sergt. * or 2 Drill Sergts.)
2 Co. Sergt. Majors (or all C.S.M's at discretion of C.O's.)
Co. Q.M. Sergts.
1 N.C.O. Bombing Instructor.
* 1 " Bayonet Instructor.
2 N.C.O's Lewis Gun Instructors.
1 N.C.O. Gas Instructor.
33% Signallers.
33% Runners.

also —
per Company — 1 Sergt., 1 Corpl. or L/Sgt., 1 L/Cpl.
(good instructors).
per Platoon — 1 Rifle bomber.
1 Scout – Sniper.
2 Lewis Gunners –
and also a few old soldiers up to 2 per Platoon.

* = "Other Special Instructors." The N.C.O's left behind should be valuable instructors.

The above is an extract from para XXX, page 58, of "Training of Divisions for Offensive Action".

MACHINE GUN COMPANY.

Up to 1 Officer per Section.
C.S.M.
4 Sergts.
2 Cpls. per Section.
3 old Soldiers per Section.

TRENCH MORTAR BATTERY.

Probably only half the Battery will go into action.

=*=*=*=*=*=*=*=*=*=*=*=*=*=

363/A

2nd. Battalion Grenadier Guards.

SHOOTING AVERAGES

			No. 1.	No. 2.	No. 3.	No. 4.
200 yds.	Slow		12.	12.28	12.3	11.72
" "	Rapid		17.3	18.64	18.2	18.2
300 "	Slow		7.4	6.16	7.3	6.75
" "	Rapid		11.6	10.13	12.1	10.31
200 "	Slow	(fixed bayonets)	12.3	12.56	13.0	12.1
" "	Rapid	{ " " }	21.4	21.37	22.7	20.57
200 "	Sp-shoot	(" ")	5.2	3.73	4.3	4.6
		Totals	85.2	84.87	89.9	84.05

Batt<u>n</u> Averages

200 slow — 12–1
— Rapid — 18–1

300 slow — 6·9
— Rapid — 11·0

Fixed Bayonets {
200 slow — 12–4
— Rapid — 21–5
— Snapshooting — 4·5
}

15th. June 1917

2nd. Battalion Grenadier Guards

Bde HQ

2nd Battalion COLDSTREAM GUARDS.

BEST SHOOTING COMPANY COMPETITION 11-12th June 1917.

	Practice 1. 100x deliberate lying – 30 secs Ray/hds	Practice 2. 100x Rapid lying – 30 secs	Practice 3. 300x deliberate lying – 10 Ray/hds	Practice 4. 300x Rapid lying – 30 secs – 30 Ray/hds	Practice 5. 200x deliberate 30 Ray/hds	Practice 6. 200x Rapid 30 Ray/hds	Practice 7. 200x snap sh. 15 secs	AVERAGE. Possible 105
No. 1 Company.	12.1	19.9	8.9	15.2	12.7	22.2	5.1	96.1
No. 2 Company.	10.8	17.1	8.8	12.2	11.3	17.9	4.4	82.5
No. 3 Company.	11.1	18.0	8.0	13.3	12.0	20.0	4.5	86.9
No. 4 Company.	12.2	19.8	9.1	14.4	12.8	21.9	4.8	95.0
Battalion Average.	11.5	18.7	8.7	13.7	12.2	20.5	4.7	90.1

Very wet all the morning ; Fair ;

No. 1 Company — Best Shooting Company

	1	2	3	4	5	6	7	
	20	30	20	30	20	30	15	= 165
Best Platoon								
No 14 Platoon No 4 Coy.	13.4	22.0	10.1	15.6	12.7	23.0	5.1	= 101.9
Best Section								
No 6 (Rifle) section 14 Platoon No 4 Coy.	15.4	24.6	10.6	17.7	14.6	(26.3)	6.4	= (115.6)
Best bombing sect.								
No 7 Sect. No 14.	10.3	18.6	9.0	16.8	11.2	22.4	7.3	= 85.6
Battalion Shot.								
Pte. Hunter (No 1 Coy)	10	28	12	28	18	(29)	6	=
Best Sergeant.								
L/Sgt. Fenton	15	26	14	23	14	26	9	= 128
Best Corporal.								
L/C. Harrison	15	(30)	15	24	16	25	9	= 134
L/C. Boswith	14	26	12	25	14	28	15	= 134
Best Sniper.								
Pte. Weddow.	18	27	10	24	15	(29)	12	= 135

◯ Good scores.

1st Guards Bde.

Herewith Battalion
Musketry averages for 11th & 12th
inst.

[Stamp: 3rd Bn. Coldstream Guards, Date 13.6.17]

Aboukir Lt & Adjt for Lt. Col.
Commanding,
3rd Bn. Coldstream Guards.

3RD BATTALION COLDSTREAM GUARDS

Company Musketry averages   11th June 1917.

Slow 200 yds   5 rounds

1	2	3	4	Battalion average
11.9	11.4	12	10.1	11.3

Rapid 200 yds   10 rounds

19.1	18.2	17.9	15.8	17.7

Slow 300 yds   5 rounds

8	8	8.3	8.6	8.2

Rapid 300 yds   10 rounds

12.7	15.3	13	12.1	13.2
51.7	52.9	51.2	46.6	50.4

Winner of Coy. Prize No. 2 Coy.

Number shooting - 709. O.R.

13/6/17.

Lt.Col.
Commanding,
3rd Battalion Coldstream Guards.

3RD BATTALION COLDSTREAM GUARDS.

Battalion Musketry Averages.　　　　　　　　12th June, 1917.

Slow. 200 Yards, fixed bayonets. 5 rounds.

No. 1 Coy.	No. 2 Coy.	No. 3 Coy.	No. 4 Coy.	Battn. Average.
12.7	11.3	12.8	12.2	12.25

Rapid. 200 Yards, fixed bayonets. 10 rounds.

21.3	19.6	21.6	19.9	20.6
34.0	30.9	34.4	32.1	32.85

Number shooting 739 O.R.

Lt. Col.,
Comdg.,
3rd Battalion Coldstream Guards.

13-6-17.

1st Battn. Irish Guards

Average Score of Battalion at each Practice on 13th & 14th June 1917

1.	2	3	4	5	6	7
200 yards SLOW. 5 rounds	200 yards RAPID 10 rounds	300 yds SLOW 5 rounds	300 yards RAPID 10 rounds	200 yds SLOW fixed bayonets 5 rounds	200 yards RAPID fixed bayonets 10 rounds	200 yards SNAPSHOOTING 5 rounds
Possible 20.	Possible 40.	Possible 20.	Possible 40.	Possible 20.	Possible 40.	Possible 15.
10.5	15.3	7.03	10.2	12.03	19.2	4.7

In the Field.
14: 6: 17.

A J Inden Lyth Bgs
for Lt. Colonel.
Comdg. 1st Battn. Irish Guards

SECRET.   Copy No. 18

1st Guards Brigade Order No. 125.

Ref. Map - HAZEBROUCK Sheet 5A.   June 7th, 1917.
          1/100,000.

1.   Battalions will move to the MORINGHEM - ZUDAUSQUES Area in accordance with attached Table to practice musketry on the TILQUES Ranges.

2.   Billeting parties will report at H.Q., of Battalions from which billets are being taken over at 12 noon on the day on which their Battalion moves.

3.   1st Line Transport not required by Battalions may be left in the present billeting Area.

4.   One old soldier per Company and one per Battalion H.Q., will remain in the present Area to look after billets.

5.   (a) Ammunition, tools, etc., may be stored in the present billets but not more than the men mentioned in para. 4, and such 1st Line Transport as O.C's. Battalions may decide, is to be left behind.

      (b) Arrangements will be made direct with Brigade Supply Officer for rationing details left behind.

6.   Ammunition, Targets, and Discs, will be provided by the Musketry School, TILQUES.

7.   A Staff Officer of the Division is billeted in the MORINGHEM - ZUDAUSQUES Area and will report at Battalion H.Q., on the arrival of Battalions in the Area to fix times and details as to the firing to be done.

8.   One lorry per Battalion has been asked for for the move each way.

      Details as to times, etc., will be notified later direct to Units concerned.

                ACKNOWLEDGE.
                                                           Captain,
                                        Brigade Major, 1st Guards Brigade.

Issued at 8 p.m.

Copy No. 1 2nd Bn. Grenadier Guards.   Copy No. 9 Guards Division, "G".
         2 2nd Bn. Coldstream Guards.   10 2nd Guards Brigade.
         3 3rd Bn. Coldstream Guards.   11 3rd Guards Brigade.
         4 1st Bn. Irish Guards.   12 S.S.O.,
         5 Bde. Machine Gun Company.   13 Area Commandant, ARQUES.
         6 Bde. Trench Mortar Battery.   14 O.C., Signals.
         7 No.3 Coy. Guards Divnl. Train.   15 Staff Captain.
         8 No.4 Field Ambulance.   16 - 18 Retained.

MARCH TABLE.

Date.	Unit.	To.	Taking over from.	Route.	Remarks.
June 10th	2/Cold.Gds.	ZUDAUSQUES - AC ACAD? de WOESTINE.	1/Scots Gds.	ARQUES - LONGUENESSE - TATINGHEM - ETREHEM.	(a) Not to arrive in billets before 5 p.m. (b) Shoot on June 11th & 12th.
	3/Cold.Gds.	HAUT SCHOMBROUCK.	3/Gren.Gds.	MORINGHEM - BARBINGHEM - GD DIFQUES.	(c) Return to present billets by same route on June 12th after shooting - to be clear of billets in MORINGHEM - ZUDAUSQUES Area by 5 p.m.
11th	2/Gren.Gds.	RENESCURE.	2/Cold.Gds.	ZUDAUSQUES - NOIRE CARME - LIHEUSE.	(a) Not to pass FORT ROUGE before 2-30 p.m. (b) Shoot on June 13th & 14th. (c) Return to present billets by same route on June 14th after shooting - to be clear of ZUDAUSQUES billets by 5 p.m. Arrangements to be made with O.C., 1/I.G. direct as to hour of march.
	1/Irish.Gds.	LA CROSSE.	3/Cold.Gds.	ARQUES - LONGUENESSE - TATINGHEM - ETREHEM. MORINGHEM - BARBINGHEM - GD DIFQUES.	(a) To be clear of FORT ROUGE by 2 p.m. (b) June on June 13th & 14th. (c) Return to present billets by same route on June 14th after shooting. To be clear of MORINGHEM billets by 5 p.m. Arrangements to be made with O.C., 2/G.G. direct as to hour of march.

SECRET.

Supplement to 1st Guards Brigade Order No.128.

June 9th, 1917.

1. Adjutants of Battalions will report to Captain E. SEYMOUR, G.S.O.3 Guards Division, on the TILQUES Ranges at 2-30 p.m. on the day on which their Battalions move to that Area. Captain SEYMOUR will then detail the course which Battalions are to fire.

2. (a) As Battalions have to start shooting at an early hour on the morning after they arrive in MORINGHEM - ZUDAUSQUES Area, the hour of march of Battalions from present Area is left to the discretion of Commanding Officers, and times laid-down in March Table issued with Order No.128 need not be adhered to.

(b) The billets in MORINGHEM - ZUDAUSQUES Area will be nearly all clear from an early hour. If incoming Units arrive before 3 p.m. and find any occupied they must bivouac until billets are clear.

(c) There is no objection to Units halting on the line of march for dinners.

(d) O.C., 2nd Bn. Grenadier Guards and O.C., 1st Bn. Irish Guards will arrange their hour of march from the present Area so that there is a distance of 1,000 yards between Battalions. *not less than*

3. Battalions will take with them their Armourer Sergeant or his Assistant.

4. Lewis Guns cannot be fired on the TILQUES Ranges.

Captain,
Brigade Major, 1st Guards Brigade.

Copies to :-
  2nd Bn. Grenadier Guards.
  2nd Bn. Coldstream Guards.
  3rd Bn. Coldstream Guards.
  1st Bn. Irish Guards.
  2nd Guards Brigade.
  3rd Guards Brigade.
  Guards Division, "G".
  Captain E.W. SEYMOUR, G.S.O. 3.

SECRET.

SECRET  Copy No. 20.

1st Guards Brigade Order No 128.

Ref. Map Sheet 27 1/40,000.
BELGIUM and FRANCE.   15th June 1917.

1. (a) The 1st Guards Brigade Group consisting of Units shown in attached March Table will move in accordance with that March Table to the OUDEZEELE - WINNIZEELE Area tomorrow June 16th.

   (b) This Group less 3rd Bn Coldstream Guards will move on June 17th to PROVEN Area.
   3rd Bn Coldstream Guards will move by bus on 17th instant to neighbourhood of DE WIPPE CABARET (1½ miles S.W. of WOESTEN.
   Orders for moves on 17th instant will be issued on evening of 16th instant.

2. Billeting parties of all Units will report to the Staff Captain at OUDEZEELE Church at 9.30 a.m. tomorrow 16th instant.

3. 1st Line Transport will move in rear of Units.

4. One lorries per Battalion and one for 1st Guards Bde. Machine Gun Coy and Trench Mortar Battery have been asked for.
   Lorries must leave present area in time or by routes so as not to interfere with movement of troops on side roads.

5. All tents in possession of Units of 1st Gds Bde will be struck and handed in to 2nd Army Troops Supply Column at ANC ABBAYE de WOESTEN before moving off. No number of tents to be handed in will be wired to this Office tonight.

6. There will be one hours halt from 11.50 a.m. to 1 p.m. during which dinners will be eaten and horses watered and fed.

7. Attention is drawn to F.S.R. Part 1. Ch.3. paras. 24 to 33.

8. Arrival in billets - position of H.Q. and numbers of men falling out will be reported to these H.Q.

9. Brigade Headquarters will close at RENESCURE at 7 a.m.
   Reports during March to head of Column.

ACKNOWLEDGE.

Issued at 6 p.m.

Captain,
Brigade Major, 1st Guards Brigade.

Copy No. 1 2nd Bn. Grenadier Guards.   Copy No.10 55th Field Coy. R.E.
        2 2nd Bn. Coldstream Guards.   11 S.A.A. Sect's.D.A.C.(2 Copi
        3 3rd Bn. Coldstream Guards.   12 Area Commandant, ARQUES.
        4 1st Bn. Irish Guards.   13 Guards Division, "G".
        5 Bde. Machine Gun Company.   14 Guards Division, "Q".
        6 Bde. Trench Mortar Battery.   15 3rd Guards Brigade.
        7 4th Guards Machine Gun Company.   16 Staff Captain.
        8 No.4 Field Ambulance.   17 O.C., Signals.
        9 No.3 Coy. Guards Divnl. Train.   18 - 20 Retained.

MARCH TABLE.

Date.	Unit and Order of March.	Starting Point.	Time.	Route.	Remarks.
June 16th.	Brigade H.Q.,	Cross Roads T.11.A.	8 a.m.	LES TROIS ROIS - ZUYTPEENE - WEMAERS Cappel - Cross Roads I.29.b. - Cross Roads J.25.b.	
	2/Cold.Gds.	—do—	8 a.m.	—do—	
	M.G.Company.	—do—	8-7 a.m.	—do—	
	T.M.Battery.	—do—	8-7 a.m.	—do—	
	1/Irish Gds.	—do—	8-10 a.m.	—do—	
	4th Guards M.G.Coy.	—do—	8-17 a.m.	—do—	
	2/Gren.Gds.	—do—	8-20 a.m.	—do—	Route to S.P. Level crossing T.15.b. - read junct. T.10.c.0.8. Not to debouch on main CASSEL Road until 1/I.G. are clear.
	3 Sections 55th Field Coy.R.E.	—do—	8-27 a.m.	—do—	To move to S.P. via RENESCURE and rd. junct. T.10.c.0.8. Not to enter RENESCURE until 2/G.G. are clear.
	No.4 Fld.Ambulance.	—do—	8-30 a.m.	—do—	To be drawn up clear of main CASSEL Road.
	No.3 Coy. Train.	—do—	8-35 a.m.	—do—	To be drawn up clear of road running from T.15.c.3.0. to T.10.c.0.8. and to debouch on main CASSEL Road in rear of 4th Fld. Amb.
	S.A.A. Sections.D.A.C.	—do—	8-37 a.m.	—do—	To move to S.P. along main CASSEL Road.
	3/Cold.Gds.	As desired.		To ZUYTPEENE thence as above.	To be clear of ZUYTPEENE by 9-15 a.m.

SECRET.

Copy No. 20

1st Guards Brigade Order No 127.

Ref. Map BELGIUM & FRANCE
Sheet 27 1/40,000.

16th June 1917.

1. (a). 1st Guards Brigade Group less 2nd Bn Grenadier Guards will continue the march tomorrow to BROVEN AREA in accordance with attached March Table.

   (b). It is probable that S.A.A. Sections, D.A.C., will move to HERZEELE; orders concerning this will be issued later.

   (c). 2nd Bn Grenadier Guards will remain in its present billets till 18th instant, when it will move to PROVEN AREA. Time of move will be notified tomorrow evening.

   (d). 3rd Bn Coldstream Guards will move with 1st Guards Brigade Group tomorrow and not by bus as previously notified. This Battalion will move on 18th instant by march route to Camp at A 10.c (Sheet 28) where it will be required to work on cable burying.

2. Billeting parties of all Units will report to the Staff Captain at Town Major's Office PROVEN at 8 a.m.

3. One Lorry per Battalion, Machine Gun Coy and Trench Mortar Battery has been asked for. Lorries must be sent off so as not to interfere with March of the column.

4. Arrival in billets, position of Headquarters, and number of men falling out, will be reported to these Headquarters.

5. Brigade Headquarters will close at WINNIZEELE at 7 a.m. Reports during march to head of column.

ACKNOWLEDGE.

Captain.
Brigade Major, 1st Guards Brigade.

Issued at :- 6.30 p.m.

Copy No 1. 2nd Bn Grenadier Guards.
2. 2nd Bn Coldstream Guards.
3. 3rd Bn Coldstream Guards.
4. 1st Bn Irish Guards.
5. 1st Gds.Bde. M.G.Coy.
6. 1st Gds.Bde. T.M.Bty.
7. 4th Guards M.G.Coy.
8. 55th Field Coy. R.E.
9. No 4 Field Ambulance.

Copy No 10. No 3 Coy. Gds.Div.Train.
11. S.A.A.Sect. D.A.C.,
12. Town Major, WINNIZEELE.
13. Guards Division "G".
14. Guards Division "Q".
15. 3rd Guards Brigade.
16. Staff Captain.
17. O.C.Signals.
18 - 20 Retained.

MARCH TABLE.

Date.	Units in order of march.	Starting Point.	Time.	Route.	Remarks.
June 17th.	No 3 Coy.Train.	Cross Roads J.12.b.9.5	7 a.m.	WATOU - Road junction E 22 b 9.2 - Cross Roads E 18 b 5.0.	An interval of 500 yards will be maintained between Units.
	Brigade H.Q.	- do -	8 a.m.	- do -	
	2/Cold. Gds.	- do -	8 a.m.	- do -	
	3/Cold. Gds.	- do -	8.15 a.m.	- do -	
	1st G.B. T.M.Bty.	- do -	8.15 a.m.	- do -	
	1st G.B. M.G.Coy.	- do -	8.30 a.m.	- do -	
	4th Guards M.G.Coy.	- do -	8.40 a.m.	- do -	
	55th Field Coy.R.E.	To join the column at WATOU at 9.40 a.m.			
	1/Irish Gds.	Cross Roads J 14 b 6.9	8 a.m.	WINNIZEELE thence as above.	
	No 4 Field Amb.	- do -	8.15 a.m.	- do -	

1st G.B. No.1239.

2nd Bn. Grenadier Guards.
2nd Bn. Coldstream Guards.
3rd Bn. Coldstream Guards.
1st Bn. Irish Guards.
Bde. Machine Gun Company.
Bde. Trench Mortar Battery.

1. The following is an Extract of Guards Division Defence Scheme :-

(a) <u>Boundaries.</u>

The front held by the Division extends from B.12.D.9.7. to B.5.D.8.8.

(b) <u>Organisation of Defence.</u>

The defensive system is organised as follows :-

(i) The front line.
(ii) The 'S' line, with supporting point at BOESINGHE CHATEAU.
(iii) The 'X' line. (The 'X' line joins the Belgian 'C' line which runs N.N.W. about 900 yards back from the Canal bank).
(iv) The 'E' line joining the Eastern defences of ELVERDINGHE to B.3.central. (This line continues Northwards in the Belgian Area).

(c) <u>Distribution of Infantry.</u>
(i) <u>Guards Brigade in the Line.</u>

Brigade Headquarters - ELVERDINGHE Chateau.
1 Battalion - Front line and 'S' line.
1 Battalion - 'X' line area.
2 Battalions - Area A.18.B. - B.13.A.& B.

(ii) <u>Liaison with the Belgians.</u>
An Officer will always be with our left Platoon on the Canal Bank.

(d) <u>Divisional Reserve.</u>
In case of attack, the Guards Brigade at PROVEN and 4th Guards M.G.Company will be prepared to march on receipt of orders to neighbourhood of DROMORE CORNER A.18.D, Brigade Headquarters moving to Divisional Headquarters in A.8.B.

2. With reference to para. d, Commanding Officers and Company Commanders will reconnoitre the Road to DROMORE CORNER and thence the Roads and tracks towards the front line.
Also the entrances of the following Communication Trenches :-
BRIDGE STR. HUNTER STR.

Commanding Officers will report when this has been done.

20th June 1917.

Captain,
Brigade Major, 1st Guards Brigade.

S E C R E T.   Copy No. 10.

368

1st Guards Brigade Order No.128.

Ref. Maps - SHEET 27 & 28. 1/40,000.   June 20th, 1917.

1.   The 2nd Bn. Grenadier Guards will move on June 24th to A.10.C. (Sheet 28) and take over the Camp at present occupied by 3rd Bn. Coldstream Guards.

2.   2nd Bn. Grenadier Guards will take over all working parties at present being found by 3rd Bn. Coldstream Guards including a Guard of 1 N.C.O. and 6 men at ONDANK R.E. Dump at A.5.d.0.7. (Sheet 28).

3.   3rd Bn. Coldstream Guards will find working parties during day of 24th; 2nd Bn. Grenadier Guards will find any required during night of 24th/25th June.

4.   Details of relief will be arranged between O.C's concerned.

5.   On relief 3rd Bn. Coldstream Guards will take over Camp at present occupied by 2nd Bn. Grenadier Guards at F.8.d. (Sheet 27).

6.   Lorries will be asked for to assist in the move.

7.   No Tents or Shelters will be removed from one Camp to the other.

ACKNOWLEDGE.

Issued at 2 p.m.

                                                          Captain,
                                    Brigade Major, 1st Guards Brigade.

Copy No. 1 2nd Bn. Grenadier Guards.
         2 3rd Bn. Coldstream Guards.
         3 Guards Division, "G".
         4 Guards Division, "Q".
         5 O.C., Corps Signals.
         6 No.3 Coy. Guards Divnl. Train.
         7 Bde. Transport Officer.
         8 O.C., Signals.
         9 Staff Captain.
        10 - 12 Retained.

369

SECRET.   Copy No. 15

1st Guards Brigade Order No. 129.

Ref. Maps - SHEET 27 & 28.
            1/40,000.   June 24th, 1917.

1.   1st Guards Brigade less 2nd Bn. Grenadier Guards will move forward to camps and bivouacs in the Area A.4. Sheet 28 and just North of it in accordance with attached March Table.

2.   1st Line Transport will move in rear of Units.

3.   Billeting Officers (with exception of 3rd Bn. Coldstream Guards) will report to Staff Captain at Brigade H.Q., at 6 p.m. to-day to receive instructions as to area to be taken over.

4.   All tents in the present area will be left standing. A guard of 1 N.C.O. and 3 men will be left in charge of the tents until the Units arrive to take them over, which will be in about 3 days time. The guard must be rationed by Units.

5.   Lorries have been asked for.
6.   Attention is drawn to Brigade Order No.355, para 1 of today 're' Traffic Routes.

7.   Brigade H.Q., will close at F.15.c.central at 2 p.m. and open at A.4.d.9.1. at same hour.

ACKNOWLEDGE.

                                                    Captain,
                        Brigade Major, 1st Guards Brigade.

Issued at 3-30 p.m.

Copy No.1 2nd Bn. Grenadier Guards.   Copy No. 8 O.C., No.3 Coy. Guards
        2 2nd Bn. Coldstream Guards.   Divisional Train.
        3 3rd Bn. Coldstream Guards.   9 Guards Division, "G".
        4 1st Bn. Irish Guards.   10 Guards Division, "Q".
        5 Bde. Machine Gun Company.   11 Area Commdt. PROVEN.
        6 Bde. Trench Mortar Battery.   12 O.C., Signals.
        7 No.4 Field Ambulance.   13 Staff Captain.
                                               14 - 16 Retained.

SCHEDULE to 1st Guards Brigade Order No.129.

Unit.	From.	To.	Starting Point and time.	Route.	Remarks.
3/Cold.Gds.	A.10.c.	A.4.c.		As convenient.	An interval of 500 yards will be maintained between Companies and every six transport vehicles.
Brigade H.Q.,2/Cold.Gds.	F.15.c.cen.	A.4.c.& 1.H.Q., 2/Cold.Gds.	F.9.c.8.9. at 2 p.m.	Military road PROVEN to LIXHOEK to point where it crosses POPERINGHE-ELVERDINGHE Road where guides from Advanced Parties must be instructed to meet Units to conduct them to Camps. Road will be policed by Brigade H.Q.	
2/Cold.Gds.	D.9.c.	A.4.c.	-do- at 9 a.m.		
1/Irish Gds.	F.14.b.	A.4.d.	-do- at 9-45 a.m.		
M.G.Company.	F.15.b.	A.4.a.	-do- at 10-30 a.m.		
T.M.Battery.	F.15.b.	A.4.a.	-do- at 10-30 a.m.		
No.4 Fld.Amb.	F.8.d.	A.4.b.	-do- at 11 a.m.		
No.3 Coy.Train.	F.14.d.	S.27.c. (Sheet 20)	-do- at 8 a.m.		

SECRET.   Copy No. **19.**

2nd Bn. Grenadier Guards.   Left Brigade.
2nd Bn. Coldstream Guards.   Right Brigade.
3rd Bn. Coldstream Guards.   Guards Division, "G".
1st Bn. Irish Guards.   75th Field Coy., R.E.
Bde. Machine Gun Company.   No.4 Field Ambulance.
Bde. Trench Mortar Battery.   Brigade Signals.
38th Divn: M.G.Company.   Brigade Bombing Officer.
Group, G.D.A.   3rd Guards Brigade.

  Herewith 1st Guards Brigade (Provisional) Defence Scheme which will come into force when relief of 2nd Guards Brigade is complete.

  APPENDICES "A" *Principles of Defence.*
      "B" Dispositions of Machine Guns.
      "C" Dispositions of Stokes Mortars.
      "D" Gas Attack and "Wind Dangerous" period.
      "E" "S.O.S"

are attached.

  Appendix "A" must be in possession of all Company Commanders and must be studied and understood by all Platoon Commanders. It will **NOT** be handed over on relief even if orders are received to hand over this Scheme. More copies of Appenidx "A" can be had on application to this Office.

  ACKNOWLEDGE.

                 Captain,

26th June 1917.   Brigade Major, 1st Guards Brigade.

1st Guards Bde Defence Scheme.
Provisional.

1. **BOUNDARIES.**

   The front held by the Division extends from B.12.d.9.7. – B.5.d.8.8.

   BOUNDARIES OF DIVISIONAL AREA.

   Northern – B.5.d.8.8. – B.5.c.5.0. West of this the boundary is not yet fixed.

   Southern – B.12.d.9.8. – B.12.d.0.4. – B.12.c.5.0. – B.18.a.0.7. – B.17.a.0.5. – B.16.a.0.2. – Road junction B.15.a.0.7. – B.8.c.0.2.

2. **ORGANIZATION OF DEFENCES.**

   The defence system is organized as follows :-

   A. The Front Line.

   B. The S Line with supporting point at BOESINGHE CHATEAU.

   C. The X Line. (This line joins the Belgian C Line which runs N.N.W. about 900 yards back from the Canal Bank).

   D. The E Line joining the Eastern defences of ELVERDINGHE to B.3. central. This line runs B.9.c.4.0. – B.9.a.4.0. – B.9.b.1.6. thence due North.

3. **DISTRIBUTION OF INFANTRY.**

   Guards Brigade in the Line.

Brigade Headquarters	–	ELVERDINGHE CHATEAU.
1 Battalion	–	(2 Coys Front Line. (1 Coy Support Line. (1 Coy Y Line & Chau. Area. (H.Q., – BOESINGHE CHATEAU (To be moved to Chasseur Fm).
1 Battalion	–	(H.Q., – BLEUET FARM. (2 Coys X Line. (2 Coys BLEUET FARM Area.
1 Battalion (In Reserve A).	–	ROUSSEL FARM – MOUTON FARM Area.
1 Battalion	–	CARDOEN FARM.
M.G. Company	–	H.Q., – MOUTON FARM. For dispositions see App."B".
T.M. Battery	–	H.Q., – EMOLE FARM. For dispositions see App."C".
Field Coy., R.E.		DECOUCK FARM.

4. **LIAISON WITH THE BELGIANS.**

   (a) One Officer will always be with the left platoon of the Brigade on the Canal Bank.

   (b) The Battalion at BLEUET FARM will send one runner to CASA BLANCA FARM and the Belgians in occupation of CASA BLANCA FARM will send one runner to BLEUET FARM.

P.T.O.

(2).

5. ARTILLERY SUPPORT.

(a) The front is supported by one Group Guards Divisional Artillery (including 1 heavy and 4 Medium Trench Mortars) with Headquarters at ELVERDINGHE CHATEAU.

A portion of the Belgian Artillery also covers the front.

(b) Support of Heavy Artillery can be called for on application to Brigade Headquarters.

(c) One Liaison Officer (F.O.O.) will be at front line Battalion H.Q., throughout the night: the O.P's at JOYEUSE FARM and ROUGE FARM will be continually manned throughout the day.

(d) S.O.S. lines are as follows :-

BABOON SUPPORT - B.12.b.8.8. - thence along the front of CANAL AVENUE - C.7.c.2.8.: the Howitzer Battery will open on the enemy's C.T's.

On an urgent call the Artillery are prepared to put down a barrage on the enemy's front line.

(e) In the event of an S.O.S. signal being made on the Brigade front, all trench mortars, including Stokes, will commence firing. Guns in the Village line will engage the enemy's approaches to their front line, especially the BOESINGHE Road and railway bridges, and the guns in the front line will engage the enemy's front line.

6. ACTION OF RESERVES IN CASE OF ATTACK.

(a) Front Line Battalion.

O.C., Front Line Battalion will act in accordance with Appendix.

(b) Supporting Battalion.

The Coys of the Supporting Battalion in the "X" Line will not be used for counter attack except under orders from Brigade H.Q.,

(c) On receipt of a wire "Defence Scheme Move."

H.Q., and 2 Coys of the Supporting Battalion will at once draw one Bandolier per man from the Brigade Store and will move from BLEUET FARM to the vicinity of LUNAVILLE FARM. They will get in touch with Brigade H.Q., on the buried cable at LUNAVILLE FARM and await orders.

O.C., Brigade Signals will send the necessary operators to LUNAVILLE FARM to fix up the communications.

(d) Battalion in Reserve "A" (ROUSSEL FARM).

The Battalion in Reserve "A" will -

(1) Send 2 companies in fighting order to man the E Line, which runs approximately B.3.central - B.9.b.1.6. - B.9.a.4.0. - B.9.c.4.0. The right of these 2 companies will rest on the ELVERDINGHE DEFENCES, the left at B.9.c.5.3. (approx).

APPENDIX "A".

PRINCIPLES OF DEFENCE.

The following principles will be adopted in holding the line :-

(a) The front line will be held as thinly as is consistent with security. To permit of thus holding the front line, good wire entanglements are necessary, good arrangements for flank defence, and close and continuous observation on the part of Artillery F.O.O's.

(b) Troops will NOT fall back from one line to any other line, but all ground will be defended as long as possible whether the flanks are turned or not.

(c) There are three kinds of attack which may be anticipated :-

    (i) A raid.

    (ii) An attack on a minor scale to capture some locality, accompanied by a bombardment.

    (iii) A serious attack preceded by a heavy bombardment.

(d) As regards (c) (i) :-

Vigilance, active patrolling, combined with a good system of listening posts and wire, make the failure of such attacks certain.

(e) As regards (c) (ii) :-

Should the enemy succeed in establishing himself in our trenches, he should be counter attacked immediately from both flanks and from the support trenches where such are in sufficiently close proximity.

The extent and intensity of the enemy's bombardment if closely observed, should give an indication of his objective and enable preparations for counter attack to be made before his attack is delivered. The essential is to deny him time in which to consolidate.

Should the counter attack fail, the captured portion of our trenches must be isolated by blocking, and support trenches firmly held until more deliberate preparations can be made.

The Infantry must do their utmost to reconnoitre and locate the exact position held by the enemy, so that our Artillery may bombard the captured trenches with precision: thus further counter attack by our reserves will be executed under the most favourable conditions.

Artillery fire will be opened on the captured trenches without the sanction of the Guards Brigadier concerned.

P.T.O.

(f) As regards (c) (iii) :-

It is unlikely that such an attack will come as a surprise, and Commanders will have time to make suitable dispositions.

In any case, no good will be gained in reinforcing the front line.

Supporting troops must hold their ground, and by means of fire and local attacks keep the enemy in check until sufficient reserves are available to assume the offensive.

(g) All Officers must consider the action to be taken by the troops under their command in the event of attack on any portion of the front for the defence of which they are responsible. Plans must be thought out beforehand, and the action to be taken known to all. Nothing should be left to chance.

Battalions and Companies must keep each other informed of their plans to meet various eventualities.

Officers Commanding Battalions in the line will always issue a Defence Scheme to their Company Commanders. This Defence Scheme should be handed over from Battalion to Battalion on relief. It should not contain any information concerning dispositions other than those of the Battalion concerned. A copy will always be sent to Brigade H.Q.,

The action to be taken by Support and Reserve Coy's. in the event of an attack should always be clearly stated, also any special tasks or special points to be defended by Lewis Guns. The action of Reserve Lewis Guns will also be laid down.

It should also be made clear that O.C., Reserve Coy's. must know the position of Units on their right and left, even though they belong to another Division or Brigade.

(2).

    (ii) Send 2 Companies to man the ELVERDINGHE DEFENCES on the perimeter of ELVERDINGHE.

    (iii) Battalion H.Q., will move to MOUTON FARM. Remaining Company will remain in billets ready to move in Fighting Order at short notice.
The Battalion in Reserve A will not be used for counter attack without reference to Divisional H.Q.,

(e) <u>Battalion in Reserve "B" (CARDOEN FARM).</u>

    The Battalion in Reserve "B" will await orders at CARDOEN FARM: it will be at short notice to move in Fighting Order.

N.B. Both Battalions in Reserve must reconnoitre the ELVERDINGHE Defences on coming into Reserve.
The following Strong Points which make up part of these defences and cover road approaches, must also be reconnoitred :-

    A.   B.14.b.3.5.
    B.   B.15.a.0.5.
    C.   B.15.c.3.6.

(f) <u>Machine Gun Company.</u>

    H.Q., of the Machine Gun Company will at once move to CHASSEUR FARM, getting in touch with Brigade H.Q., through the H.Q., of the Front Line Battalion.
The three guns in reserve will occupy prepared positions in the X Line.

(g) <u>Machine Gun Company (additional).</u>

    The Machine Gun Company of 38th Division will man emplacements as follows :-
        4 Guns in ELVERDINGHE.
        2 Guns in L.2. (B.23.)
        1 Gun at PARROY FARM (B.16.d.0.5.)
        1 Gun at BAKERY BARN (B.15.d.)

Eight guns will move from A.10.d.1.1., four of which will occupy emplacements in houses A, B, C of the ELVERDINGHE DEFENCES, the remaining four moving to Brigade H.Q., as Brigade Reserve.
The O.C., Machine Gun Company will report at Brigade H.Q.,

(h) The Field Coy. will remain at DECOUCK FARM and await orders.

(i) H.Q., and two reserve guns of the Trench Mortar Battery will move to LUNAVILLE FARM, and await orders.

7. <u>WORKING PARTIES.</u>
In the event of attack all working parties will come under the orders of the nearest Battalion Commander at whose H.Q. they will report.

8. <u>BOMB and AMMUNITION STORES.</u>
The main Brigade Bomb and Ammunition Stores is near BLEUET FARM: on the road at B.10.c.15.0.
There are emergency stores in BRIDGE STREET at BOUSSAT FARM (B.10.b.5.0.) - in HUNTER STREET at CHASSEUR FARM (B.11.d.3.2.)
There is also a store in ELVERDINGHE CHATEAU.

9. <u>R.E. DUMP</u>
The R.E. Dump from which Battalions draw direct is at the Gasometer, ELVERDINGHE, B.15.a.3.7½.

1st. G.B. No.1344.
26/6/1917.

                            Captain.
          Brigade Major, 1st Guards Brigade.

APPENDIX "B".

DISPOSITIONS OF MACHINE GUNS.

B.5.1.	at B.5.b.0.6.	firing E.S.E.
B.5.2.	at B.6.c.0.1.	firing N.W.
B.12.1.	at B.12.d.8.8.	firing S.E.
B.12.2.	at B.12.b.0.1.	firing E.
B.12.3.	at B.12.b.1.1.	firing E.
B.12.4.	at B.12.a.6.5.	firing N.N.W.
B.12.5.	at B.12.d.5.1.	firing N.
B.12.6.	at B.12.c.1.1.	firing N.N.W.
B.11.4.	at B.11.d.5.6.	firing N.W.
B.11.3.	at B.11.a.3.4.	firing S.E.
B.11.2.	at B.11.b.8.8.	firing N.E.
B.11.1.	at B.11.a.6.5.	firing N.E.

Main Street B.12.a.2.6. firing N.E.

Two guns at CHASSEUR FARM in readiness to occupy positions in the X Line.

One gun at MOUTON FARM.

—:*:—

APPENDIX "C".

DISPOSITIONS OF STOKES MORTARS.

B.12.a.7½.3.
B.12.a.7.5.
B.12.a.6.5½.
B.12.a.5.5.
B.6.c.1.1.
B.6.c.½.½.

POSITION OF HEAVY T.M.

B.11.b.8½.8.

DISPOSITIONS OF MEDIUM T.M's.

B.12.b.0.7½. firing S.E. - E.S.E.

B.12.a.8.8. firing E.N.E. into the road and BABOON LANE.

B.12.b.0.½. firing N.N.E. into the road bridge.

B.12.a.7.2. firing E.N.E. into the railway bridge.

—:*:—

P.T.O.

APPENDIX "D".

GAS ATTACK and "WIND DANGEROUS" PERIOD.

The orders contained in Second Army G.221 (Instructions for wind dangerous period and action during gas attack) will be adhered to in every detail.

East of the line - ELVERDINGHE WOESTEN, Box Respirators will always be carried in the ready position, whether wind is dangerous or not.

APPENDIX "E".

S.O.S.

The "S.O.S" telephone message or "S.O.S" rocket signal, means that the Germans are actually leaving their trenches to attack, and that rapid barrage is required from guns and from Machine Guns that can barrage in front of our front line.

-:*:-

SECRET.

1st Guards Brigade Order No.130.

Ref. Maps - ELVERDINGHE, 1/10,000.   June 27th, 1917.
        ST. JULIEN,
        BIXSCHOOTE,

1.   1st Guards Brigade will relieve 2nd Guards Brigade in the BOESINGHE Sector on June 28th and 29th in accordance with attached Table.
       Further details of relief will be arranged direct between O.C's concerned.

2.   1st Line Transport will take over lines vacated by Units of 2nd Guards Brigade.

3.   No lorries are available for the move.
       Details not going into the trenches will probably be accommodated in a separate Camp. Orders concerning this will be issued later.

5.   Secret Trench Maps, Intelligence, Aeroplane Photographs, etc., will be taken over.

6.   Completion of relief will be reported by Second Army Trench Code to Brigade H.Q.,

7.   G.O.C., 1st Guards Brigade, will take over command of BOESINGHE Sector at 4 p.m. on 29th, until which hour all Units of 1st Guards Brigade in the 2nd Guards Brigade Area will come under Orders of G.O.C., 2nd Guards Brigade.

8.   Brigade H.Q., will close at A.4.d.9.2. and open at ELVERDINGHE CHATEAU at 4 p.m. on June 29th.

ACKNOWLEDGE.

                                              Captain,
               Brigade Major, 1st Guards Brigade.

Issued at 6 a.m.

Copy No.1 2nd Bn. Grenadier Guards.   Copy No.9 2nd Guards Brigade.
     2 2nd Bn. Coldstream Guards.   10 75th Field Coy. R.E.
     3 3rd Bn. Coldstream Guards.   11 No.3 Coy. Guards Divnl.
     4 1st Bn. Irish Guards.   Train.
     5 Bde. Machine Gun Company.   12 Bde. Transport Offr.,
     6 Bde. Trench Mortar Battery.   13 O.C., Signals.
     7 Guards Division, "G".   14 Staff Captain.
     8 Guards Division, "Q".   15 - 17 Retained.

Date.	Unit.	From.	To.	Taking over from.	Remarks.
June 28th.	3/Cold.Gds.	A.4.c.	Front and Support Line.	3/Gren.Gds.	Leading platoons to pass CARDOEN FARM at 9-30 p.m. Guides – 1 per platoon and Bn. H.Q. will meet Battalion at CARDOEN FARM.
"	1/Irish.Gds. T.M.Battery.	A.4.d. S.27.c. (Sheet 20.)	RUSSEL FARM. Line.	1/Cold.Gds. 2nd Guards Bde. T.M.Battery.	Leading platoon to leave Camp at 2 p.m. Arrangements direct. Relief to be complete by 8 p.m. G.S. Wagon from Bde.H.Q. as required.
29th.	Brigade H.Q.	A.4:d.9.2.	ELVERDINCHE CHATEAU.	2nd Guards Bde. H.Q.	
"	3/Gren.Gds.	DE WIPPE cross rds.	CARDOEN FARM.	1/Scots Gds.	To work on day of 29th. Leading platoon to arrive CARDOEN FARM 6 p.m. Details of work and guard at ONDANK Dump to be handed over to 1/S.G. who will work on cable burying on night 29th/30th.
"	2/Cold.Gds.	A.4.c.	Line and BLEUET FM:	2/Irish Gds.	Loading platoon to pass CARDOEN FM: at 9-30 p.m. Guides – 1 per platoon and Bn. H.Q. at CARDOEN FM: 1.Officer and 1.N.C.O. per Company to report at BLEUET FM: at 6 p.m. on 28th to remain for night and take over work in hand.
"	M.G.Company.	S.20.d.	Line.	2nd Guards Bde. M.G.Company.	Relief to be complete by 6 p.m.

N.B. All movement will be by Platoons at 200 yards interval.
Transport vehicles moving South or East of DE WIPPE CABARET cross roads will move in pairs at 200 yards interval.

Intelligence Report - 1st Guards Brigade.

11 a.m. June 29th to 11 a.m. June 30th.

OPERATIONS. Trench Mortar Battery fired 160 rounds and carried out registration.

Three periscopes were smashed as well as two dummy periscopes.

The enemy fired occasionally throughout the day and night. He made one lucky hit in the night.

INTELLIGENCE.

Movement was noticed as folows :-
A few sentries in enemy front line.
Three men in ARTILLERY WOOD during the morning.
Two men rear a farm at C.1.a.1.7.
Eleven men who came down the old railway track. These men were unarmed, and appeared to be in charge of a twelvth man who carried rifle and fixed bayonet. This man marched in rear of the party. The men disappeared from view but were observed a little later carrying large pieces of timber down a trench leading towards ARTILLERY WOOD.

A sentry was seen in what looks like a concrete emplacement on the North side of STEAM MILL.

One German seen getting through hedge at C.1.c.3.3. at 4-40 p.m. going east.

Work. Earth was being thrown out of a trench round the HILL during the afternoon.

No work whatever appears to be taking place in the front line, not was there any sound of working parties during the night.

A large camouflage sheet partly concealed by branches, covers what appears to be a large dump of R.E. material at C.1.a.7.2. (about) T. B 20° from B.12.c.3.5.

In rear of this there is a large emplacement of some sort on the edge of the wood.

ARTILLERY.

Both sides were very active all day.
BOESINGHE was shelled during the morning by a 5.9 gun shooting from the direction of LANGEMARCK.

ARTILLERY WOOD was heavily shelled by our heavies and several dugouts had direct hits - but one or two strong looking positions on the South corner did not appear to be hit at all.

The enemy seldom fires any field guns.
At 3-45 a.m. hostile artillery shelled the X Line with 4.2's. One direct hit. Shelling ceased at 4-10 a.m.
In afternoon and evening of 29th enemy artillery heavily shelled the track in B.9.c. doing a lot of damage to the road.

AIRCRAFT.

Very active from noon onwards.
At 12-55 p.m. 5 of ours engaged with four E.A. The enemy appeared to be driven off: one E.A. dropped a small red balloon.

At 1 p.m. one of our observing machines was hit by a shell and fell in flames.

At 6-30 p.m. two E.A's. painted white flew very low over the lines. They returned later accompanied by 4 red planes.

At 8-15 p.m. 22 enemy planes were over our lines; 4 of these kept very low and were obviously finding out what was going on in our front line.

An observation balloon was sent up at 3 p.m. T B 65° from B.12.a.3.5. Following this ascent positions in our near were heavily shelled.

Lieut.,
for Brigade Major 1st Guards Brigade.

www.ingramcontent.com/pod-product-compliance
Lightning Source LLC
Chambersburg PA
CBHW081458160426
43193CB00013B/2531